Gratitude CHANGES Everything

journal belongs to... !

Thank You !

www.annettebridges.com

ISBN: 978-1-946371-12-6

Gratitude CHANGES Everything

1. Begin your gratitude journal by listing everything you can think of that makes you grateful. Start with the ability to breath.

2. What skills or abilities are you thankful to have?

3. How is where you are in life today different than a year ago — and what positive changes are you thankful for?

4. What are you taking for granted about your day to day that you can be thankful for?

5. List people in your life who are hard to get along with — and write down at least one quality for each that you are grateful for.

6. Which season are you most grateful for and why?

7. Write about a time you were grateful for something a friend did for you.

8. Write about a pet you are grateful for.

9. What are three ways to say "thank you" without using the words thank you?

10. Pause for a moment. What are you grateful for right here, right now.

11. Write a thank you card to your self and name three things you can thank yourself for.

12. What made you smile today?

13. Go outside. What are three things you see that you are grateful for?

14. Name three things in your home you are grateful for.

15. Describe the feeling of thankfulness.

16. What is your favorite Thanksgiving memory?

17. Something I am grateful for that has been hard for me …

18. Something I am grateful for that makes me happy …

19. How does it feel to be thanked?

20. Who are you most thankful for?

21. Write down your favorite part of the day and why you are grateful for it.

22. Watch a sunrise or sunset. Write about how you felt and your feelings of thankfulness.

23. Who was the last person you hugged? Write about why you are grateful for them.

24. Think of a song that puts you in a good mood, and write about how amazing it is that you can hear something so beautiful and how this song makes you feel.

25. Write about something in your life that you love doing the most, and why you are grateful you are able to do it.

26. What is your favorite emotion to feel and why?

27. What do you love most about life? And why?

28. Go outside with your journal and write about how good it feels to be out in nature and all the positive feelings it brings you.

29. What's the most beautiful thing you saw today?

30. Each evening before you go to bed, list five things you are grateful for from the day.

color your world

ABOUT the CREATOR

Annette Bridges is an author, publisher and women's retreat host on a mission to help every woman realize her story is extraordinary, valuable and noteworthy.

She has published the *Color Your World Journal Series* and formed a journal club to provide community, support and tools for women to record their ideas, feelings, experiences, memories and all the important details of their lives.

Before writing books and publishing journals and coloring books, this former public school and homeschool educator spent a decade writing hundreds of helpful, instructive, and light-hearted columns published by Texas newspapers, parenting magazines, websites and bloggers.

Annette lives on a Texas cattle ranch with her husband John, dachshund Lady and lots of cows. She can drive a tractor but only if wearing a fresh coat of lipstick and it's not her pedicure day!

You can learn more about Annette's books and products, blogs and videos as well as her women's retreats and other events at www.annettebridges.com.

Look for her on social media, too!

MESSAGE from the PUBLISHER

The *Color Your World Journal Series* is a pathway to self-discovery. It's where you write notes to yourself. Be your own cheerleader. Give yourself encouragement. Tell yourself what you're grateful for. Celebrate you!

There are countless reasons to keep a journal including collecting favorite recipes, listing goals and celebrating every experience and every one that's near and dear to you. A journal provides a home for the memories and lessons learned that you never want to forget.

Why a niche journal?

If you're anything like me, you have a journal (or even two or three journals) where you write anything and everything about anything and everything. My challenge comes when trying to find something I've written. I flip and flip through the pages of my two, three or four journals trying to find whatever it is. I never remember which journal I wrote down my whatever's!!

The solution? A niche journal! A journal that has a specific focus and theme! A journal where you can record your ideas, inspirations and things you want to remember in the appropriate journal.

Why big unlined paper?

Because big unlined paper is needed to record big ideas, dreams and memories! You need room to grow, stretch and expand. You need space to think beyond the confines of what you've always done, to pursue new dreams, discover your power and reimagine your purpose again and again. You need pages without lines and limitations to reconnect with your creative, perfectly imperfect self.

Plus, big unlined paper gives you space for more than words. You have plenty of room to doodle, draw or post photographs and clippings, too.

Why color is important?

When you journal, use colored pens and markers! Your world doesn't happen in black and white. Your life should be lived and written about in many colors. Even dark and sad memories feel lighter and brighter when told in color.

Journaling in color affects your mood and perception of your world. Colors evoke calm, cheer and comfort. Using color can lift your spirit and inspire your imagination. You may be surprised by all the beautiful benefits from adding more color into your life story.

When journaling, give yourself time to listen to your heart and reflect. Breathe in the moments. Feel. Be quiet. Let yourself be totally and thoroughly present with your thoughts. Let your heart transform you and teach you new insights. Open your mind to consider new ideas and possibilities. You may find that what your heart teaches will be life changing.